Compliments of

FIRST ALLIANCE CORPORATION

Corporate Headquarters ★ City Hall Plaza ★ 900 Elm Street ★ 10th Floor ★ Manchester ★ NH 03101
ph(603)628-1298 ★ fx(603)625-5650

NEW HAMPSHIRE
LIFE

NEW HAMPSHIRE
LIFE

PHOTOGRAPHS FROM

The Union Leader

AND

New Hampshire Sunday News

Produced for the

Union Leader Corporation

by

Peter E. Randall Publisher

Portsmouth, New Hampshire

1995

From the Publisher

Welcome to a celebration of life in New Hampshire.

Since acquiring a new Flexographic press in 1990, *The Union Leader* and *New Hampshire Sunday News* have published thousands of color images of people at work and at play in the state we love.

It was an easy decision to put some of those pictures in book form so that you might enjoy them at your leisure. The tough part was in choosing which pictures to use.

New Hampshire is a very special state. It offers us so much to enhance our daily lives. These pictures are guaranteed to refresh your own favorite memories of New Hampshire and her people — from bubbling brooks and salty beaches to laughing children and thoughtful adults.

Our hope is that you enjoy looking through this book as much as we enjoyed putting it together for you.

Nackey S. Loeb

Additional copies available from The Union Leader, Box 9555, Manchester, N.H. 03108-9555.

Produced by Peter E. Randall Publisher, Box 4726, Portsmouth, NH 03802-4726
Design by Tom Allen

Photos on previous pages:
Charlie A. Moulton of New Hampton's Ancestral Acres farm has Robb, his two-year-old border collie, for company as he gathers maple sap. Photo by Jeanne Morris

Sunset on Lake Massabesic. Photo by Bob LaPree

The Old Man of the Mountain. Photo by Dave Burroughs

Printed in Canada

ISBN 0-9648921-0-3

The Photographers

Bob LaPree, of Contoocook, started taking pictures in junior high and began working as a news photographer in 1971. He has done assignments for national publications and the Associated Press and was staff photographer for the *New Hampshire Times* and chief videographer at WMUR-TV. He joined *The Union Leader* in 1986.

The U.S. Army switched his orders, which is how **George Naum** began a photography career that has spanned a half-century. He was on hand for the opening of the Korean peace talks in 1951 and joined *The Union Leader* later that year. His family includes his wife Sadie, two daughters and a son.

Dick Morin began taking pictures as a student for the Manchester West High School newspaper. He managed department store camera departments and was a wedding photographer before joining *The Union Leader* in 1971. His favorite subjects: kids at play, sports, and the political scene.

David Burroughs   **John Clayton**   **Jeanne Morris**   **Shawne K. Wickham**

David Burroughs' primary duties for *The Union Leader* are as a photo lab technician...John Clayton is best known for his "In the City" columns, which have been published in book form...Jeanne Morris and Shawne K. Wickham are reporter-photographers for the *New Hampshire Sunday News*.

Also contributing photographs to this book were independent news correspondents Lorna Colquhoun, Roger Amsden, and Mike Manzo, along with *Sunday News* staffers Denis Paiste and Roger Talbot.

Just waiting for someone to row it, a boat sits on the Suncook River of an early morning in Pittsfield.
Photo by Dave Burroughs

A seagull and the spire of St. Marie Church on Manchester's West Side are silhouetted as the sun sets behind Mt. Uncanoonuc in nearby Goffstown. Photo by Bob LaPree

A time-lapse picture adds even more color, or so it seems, to a carnival's Ferris wheel ride along Manchester's riverfront.
Photo by Bob LaPree

The state's two tallest buildings cast their light upon the dark waters of the Merrimack River on a fall night. The Hampshire Plaza is at left. Its slightly taller neighbor is the NYNEX building. Photo by Bob LaPree

Previous pages: Hot air balloons rise out of the morning mist of the Suncook River in Pittsfield.. Photo by Dave Burroughs

Spring rushes at you from below the Waterloo Bridge on the Warner River. The bridge, circa 1840, was rebuilt by the town in 1972. Photo by Bob LaPree

Frozen in time, and just frozen. Hampton Beach (left) is the spot to be on a hot day. And even a simple branch takes on a beauty after a winter storm in Manchester.
Photos by Dick Morin (left) and George Naum

Manchester's West Side and millyard area are illuminated by the rockets' red glare on an Independence eve. That's the Notre Dame bridge in foreground. Photo by Bob LaPree

Opposite: Colonial times come back to life when militia units are on parade in New Hampshire. Photo by John Clayton

Top: Stephen Gasiorowski is part of the Yankee Brass Band Festival, which uses antique instruments to play tunes popular in the 1800s. Photo by George Naum

Bottom: A century earlier is celebrated by the New Hampshire Regiment, whose members marched in Milford's bicentennial parade on July 2, 1994, despite 90-degree heat. Photo by Shawne K. Wickham

Top: Jennifer Hornbeck, 9, Kylie Hornbeck, 5, and Holly Kee, 12, came from Laconia to join a rally at Veterans Park in Manchester in support of U.S. troops in the Gulf War on Feb. 9, 1991.
Photo by Dick Morin

Bottom: Children from a Manchester day-care center had plenty of flags to wave during a 1993 Veterans Day parade on Elm Street, Manchester. Photo by Jeanne Morris

Strawbery Banke staff member Elizabeth Nowers of Somersworth participated in the Portsmouth museum's first-ever Thanksgiving traditions event in 1993. Photo by George Naum

Is that really Keyran Walsh, 18th century sea captain, gazing out a window at Strawbery Banke? Or might it be Patrick Richard of Portsmouth, a role-player at the interpretive museum? Photo by Shawne K. Wickham

Oscar Ladd was 91 when, as Orford's oldest resident, he received the town's Boston Post cane in 1990. The canes have long outlived the newspaper that dreamed them up as a publicity stunt. Photo by Denis Paiste

Opposite: Hampton Harbor's clam flats had been closed for six years and Nicholas Addorid of Portsmouth was on hand bright and early for the reopening in October of 1994. Photo by Jeanne Morris

Sea of grass. Jim Cates' parrot, Sam, is just along for the ride as the lawn gets mowed on Candia Road, Manchester.
Photo by Bob LaPree

Lori Langway of Manchester has an armful of toys for the annual Salvation Army Toy Run put on by New Hampshire motorcyclists. Photo by John Clayton

Boy's toy. William Berthiaume of Manchester is rightly proud of his 1933 Chevy coupe, sporting a 350 V-8 with dual carburetors. Photo by Bob LaPree

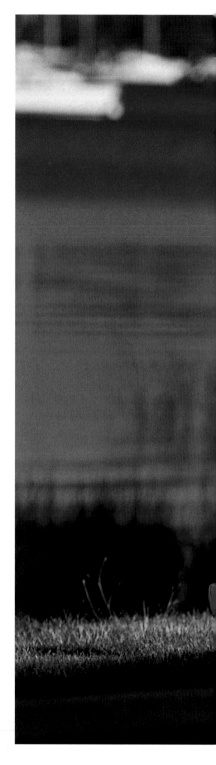

Late-day sun, the lapping of the waves of Massabesic Lake, a good book, and good company. That's plenty for Florence and Joe Barriss of Derry. Photo by Bob LaPree

Author Ronald Jager spends some quiet time in the backyard of his 18th century farmhouse in Washington. His book Last House On The Road, *was published in 1994. Photo by Mike Manzo*

Opposite: Old Man Winter. In Manchester's Bronstein Park, a familiar figure stands, despite the cold and blowing snow. Robert Wade regularly declines offers for indoor shelter. Photo by Jeanne Morris

As Hurricane Bob made good his escape on Aug. 19, 1991, thrill-seekers ran across Hampton Beach to check the surf. Photo by George Naum

Tamer showers, courtesy of a Manchester Fire Department hose, are to the liking of Sarah Bouchard, 6, and friends at Piscataquog Park. Photo by George Naum

It's three-in-a-row at a water slide set up at Plymouth State College's annual picnic for employees and families. Photo by Dick Morin

Opposite : Manchester's Fun in the Sun program is even more fun in the spray from a fire department truck on a hot and hazy summer's day. Photo by George Naum

Jill Prentis of Manchester Central High's marching band puts her music where her mouth is — on her flute.
Photo by Dick Morin

Opposite: Clown clones? Elizabeth Bornstein, 5, of Bow seems to have met her match in Pockets (Michael Wexler) during a
Purim celebration at Temple Adath Yeshurun, Manchester. Photo by John Clayton

A face only a mother could love looks like a prize-winner for sure at the Stratham Fair pie-eating contest.
Photo by Dick Morin

Opposite: Mat Cote, 9, of Manchester, has his eye on his marble game on a basketball court at Livingston Park in the Queen
City. Photo by Bob LaPree

Eighth-graders in a Hooksett Memorial School science class used Mylar glasses to protect their eyes while watching the annular eclipse of the sun May 10, 1994. Photos by Dick Morin (above) and Bob LaPree

Rollin' on the river. Anthony Paquet of Suncook gets a rollerblade workout while son Trevor enjoys the view along the Merrimack River at Arms Park, Manchester. Photo by Bob LaPree

Kirby Johns of Durham, front, Laini Fallon of Strafford, center, and Chie Thibodeau of Lee, rear, freshen their makeup before a "Nutcracker" dress rehearsal at UNH's Johnson Theater, Durham.

Being a bunny can be scary. Three among 80 "Nutcracker" performers await their turn. Photos by Jeanne Morris

A National Guard volunteer salutes Dagmar Pearson, 23, of Chocorua, a gold medalist at the New Hampshire Special Olympics Summer Games in Durham. Photo by Roger Talbot

Opposite: A midday summer's dream seems to entrance Amelia Gardner, 8, of Warner, who holds a graceful position while fishing beside the Warner River. Photo by Roger Amsden

Here, Washington listens to its citizens. Moderator Mike Otterson, left, oversees the annual Town of Washington meeting as resident Jim Hofford, standing at right, makes a point.

Opposite: Emily Rumrill, right, watches as Assistant Town Moderator Robert Crane II deposits her ballot while Janice Philbrick checks her off the voting list. Photos by Bob LaPree

Are three heads better? Larry, left, and Don Gaskill confer with Clinton Cornell over the Washington town report.
Photo by Bob LaPree

Pondering a point of order is former Milford School Board chairman Ernest Barrett at the school district meeting.
Photo by Jeanne Morris

New Hampshire worships. The East Washington Congregational Church beckons from atop a rise (opposite page). Altar server Danny Anctill (left) extinguishes candles during a Good Friday service at St. Joseph Cathedral, Manchester. Lighting a giant menorah during Chanukah celebrations (below) at the Jewish Federation in Manchester is Brian Goodman.
Photos by Bob LaPree

Sandy Lockwood of Milford is a swirl of color at the Center of New Hampshire Holiday Inn, one of several sites for a New England Square and Round Dance convention that drew 5,000 dancers. Photo by Dick Morin

What's a New Hampshire fair without food? Fred Demming grills sausages, peppers and onions at the annual Lancaster Fair.
Photo by Lorna Colquhoun

Rocky Hyndman is a professional shoe shiner in Manchester who goes to his customers. Here he puts a gloss on Don Kingsbury's shoes in a local pub.

Opposite: Fortier, farrier. Diane Fortier of Henniker trims the hoof of a miniature purebred named Story Book Peter Pan. Fortier also shoes full-sized horses, cows, goats, and llamas.
Photos by Bob LaPree

Where is Boston's Air Route Traffic Control Center? In Nashua, New Hampshire, of course. That's controller Mark Sheehy, left, and radar associate Tim Rivers. Photo by Bob LaPree

"I touch the stars," said teacher-astronaut Christa McAuliffe, whose memory lives on in the McAuliffe Planetarium, Concord, where production specialist Lynn Rice controls the show. Photo by George Naum

Workers from a Worcester, Massachusetts, firm prepare New Hampshire's State House dome for a facelift and a new coat of 23.5-karat golf leaf. Photo by Bob LaPree

Samantha Beaulieu carries five plates at once while waiting on patrons at a sports bar in Manchester.
Photo by Bob LaPree

New Hampshire Symphony Orchestra timpanist Jeffrey Fischer is all concentration. Photo by Bob LaPree

Richard C. Bresnahan works up a sweat as he puts his Manchester Central High School band members through their paces before an annual spring concert. Photo by Bob LaPree

Working together, volunteers in the Fall Mountain Regional school district get ready to raise the frame of a new classroom.
Photo by Shawne K. Wickham

Glenn Silley of Franklin climbs the Rumney Cliffs, which a rock-climbing group has bought to turn over to the U.S. Forest Service. Photo by Jeanne Morris

Trying his luck, in more ways than one, a boy fishes a pond in Peterborough. Photo by Dave Burroughs

Opposite: Still wild, Scott's Brook flows into the Second Connecticut Lake in New Hampshire's far North Country. Here, a boy learns the art of trout fishing. Photo by Bob LaPree

Ice fishing with Brandy, his golden retriever, on Crystal Lake in Manchester is Ken Cayer of Candia. Photo by Dick Morin

Previous pages: What better way to see New Hampshire's White Mountain scenery than in a sail plane? Walter Kyle of Franconia Soaring Center has a distinguished backseat driver in U.S. District Court Judge Steven J. McAuliffe. Photo by Jeanne Morris

Let the snow melt just enough to clear the court and New Hampshire teens will play a little basketball. These Hopkinton High students play at Georges Park, Contoocook. Photo by Bob LaPree

David Livingston of Goffstown seems to be about to make contact with the camera lens in this shot from frozen Lake Massabesic in Auburn. Photo by Dick Morin

A windsurfer is on his way on Great Bay, Newington. Photo by Dave Burroughs

Give a New Hampshire boy a board and a hill, and stand clear! Jeffrey Correa uses his snowboard in the traditional way on a cold day at Gossler Park School in Manchester. Without snow, a Concord sandpit is good enough for Garth Olson to catch some air while friend Derek See readies for takeoff. Photos by John Clayton (snow) and Dick Morin

A kayaker is silhouetted by the late afternoon sun on the slalom course at Arms Park on the Merrimack River in Manchester. Photo by Bob LaPree

Previous pages: David Mitchell of Canaan races through the slalom course during a Kayak Master event, part of the Mad River Canoe New England Slalom Series. Photo by Dick Morin

Oarsman Mike Fonner has a tough row to hoe as he leads a four-man crew from the Amoskeag Club through a morning workout on the Merrimack. Photo by John Clayton

Keeping his head down is Ed Vallee of Rochester, during a break from the annual State Amateur Golf Tournament. Golf continues to gain in popularity in the Granite State.

Opposite page: Jane Nowlin of the Country Club of New Hampshire lets her ball know she isn't pleased after it fails to drop during a state golf association championship at Portsmouth Country Club. Photos by George Naum

Concord High's Sandy Washburn is just a bit ahead of Dover's Sarah Jolly in this battle for a loose ball in a schoolgirl soccer game.

Opposite page: Long jumper Tony Trisciani of Manchester Memorial High School strains for every inch in decathlon competition at Nashua. Photos by Dick Morin

What would Little League be in New Hampshire without a little rain? These Bedford moms (top) weather things nicely. Popcorn makes watching more fun, and Kyle Riffe, age 2, of South Berwick, Maine, had both on a summer evening at Concord's Memorial Field Photos by Bob LaPree

Opposite: Members of the Pinkerton Academy football team of Derry celebrate a state championship victory, the school's fourth straight. Photo by Dick Morin

It must be the hills. New Hampshire produces some of the nation's finest cross-country runners, many of whom compete on Manchester's tough Derryfield Park course. Photo by Dick Morin

Right: Nearly 3,000 runners crowd the starting line at a Healthsource road race on Elm Street on a summer evening. Photo by Bob LaPree

What would you call a black Labrador who helps you pan for gold? Willie Ford of Charlestown's friend is Nugget, naturally.
Photo by Lorna Colquhoun

The Crane Farm in Washington has been producing maple syrup for more than 100 years. Jeanette Crane tends the wood-fired boiling pan. Photo by Bob LaPree

Lilacs, New Hampshire's state flower, catch the sun's rays. Photo by George Naum

Lady slippers stand in a spruce forest near Third Connecticut Lake in Pittsburg. Photo by Bob LaPree

With the forsythia in bloom, spring is surely coming. This house sits near the corner of Beech and Harrison streets on Manchester's East Side. Photo by George Naum

*A flower basket on a stump …
a seasonally-decorated doorway
… Granite Staters like to deco-
rate their environs. Photos by
George Naum*

His "friend" doesn't talk much, but that's OK with Xenophon Christous of East Manchester, who lets his terraced flower garden speak for itself. Photo by John Clayton

Fresh corn, anyone? Who can resist Lisa Mason Seward's offering from Clark's Farm, Bedford?
Photo by George Naum

How do you like them apples? They are ripe for the picking at Hackleboro Orchards in Canterbury. Photo by Roger Amsden

Opposite: Even a city street on Manchester's West Side comes alive with fall colors when the maples turn. Photo by George Naum

Concord farmer Abbot Presby moves a wheelbarrow load of pumpkins at his Dimond Hill Farm stand. His stock includes 11 varieties of pumpkins, eight of winter squash, and more. Photo by Bob LaPree

That's a Great Pumpkin! And it belongs to James Kuhn Sr., who grew the 593 1/2 pounder in his Goffstown garden.
Photo by Bob LaPree

It is downright scary how everyone pitches in at harvest time in New Hampshire. A ghost sits behind the wheel of an old farm tractor at the Paul LaPierre home on Rundlett Hill Road, Bedford. Photo by George Naum

Opposite: New Hampshire folk like to celebrate the seasons. Lea Devriendt lights one of 223 jack-o-lanterns that she and friends displayed at her Goffstown home. Photo by Bob LaPree

Seconds, anyone? An odd pairing of items for sale catches the eye, if not the palate, at Champny's Market in Bow. Photo by Dick Morin

Opposite: Pumpkins galore beckon at the "Beans & Greens" roadside stand on Rte. 11B in Gilford. Photo by George Naum

Santa Claus can't be everywhere, so Milton Davis helps him wish a Merry Christmas to all by decorating the Davis home at 1728 Candia Road in Manchester. Photo by Bob LaPree

A Christmas tree in front of the Memorial Arch at the State House in Concord adds a holiday gleam to a December's evening. Photo by Bob LaPree

A loon cruises the East Inlet of Second Connecticut Lake near Pittsburg, at the northern tip of New Hampshire.
Photo by Bob LaPree

A great blue heron searches for prey on a late October afternoon near the shore of Lake Massabesic in Auburn.
Photo by Bob LaPree

Horse-pulling contests are a big draw at New Hampshire fairs. This one took place at the annual Stratham Fair.
Photo by Dick Morin

Pleasure horses are a big part of New Hampshire life. Here new life is nurtured as Honey for the Bees nuzzles her newborn colt, Junior, at Brindle Ledge Farm, Goffstown. Photo by Dick Morin

He is the egg man. Bert Southwick has been home-delivering eggs in Tilton and Northfield via horse and wagon since 1937. Photo by Roger Amsden

A bull moose grazes along Route 3 at "Moose Alley" near the Connecticut Lakes. Photo by Bob LaPree

The photographer's dog, a samoyed named Shardik, helped illustrate a story on how to keep pets cool in hot weather. Photo by Shawne K. Wickham

Two cats have their own view of things from the windows of the Main Street, New Castle home of Dave Champagne.
Photo by George Naum

New Hampshire Audubon Society naturalist Scott Fitzgerald and Sage, a one-winged barred owl under the society's care.
Photo by Dick Morin

Birds of a feather have friends in Leo and Kim Hebert of Merrimack, who feed orphaned birds that people bring to them from miles around. Photo by Shawne K. Wickham

"Get off of my face," the Old Man of the Mountain might be saying as caretaker David Nielsen of Gilmanton makes his way down the granite brow, high above Franconia Notch. Then again, the Old Man might be grateful for the facial.
Photo by Lorna Colquhoun